Prayers for Others

Prayers of Intercession
by
Michael Hollings
&
Etta Gullick

MAYHEW-McCRIMMON
Great Wakering Essex

First Published in 1977
by Mayhew-McCrimmon Great Wakering Essex

© Copyright 1977 by Michael Hollings
and Etta Gullick

ISBN 0 85597 229 7

Cover design: Russell North

ACKNOWLEDGEMENTS

The authors and the publishers wish to express their gratitude to the
following for permission to include copyright material in this book:

Fontana Publications, Wm Collins Sons & Co. Ltd for a prayer from
Plain Man's Book of Prayers by William Barclay.

S.L.G. Press, Oxford for a prayer by Gilbert Shaw.

Church Pastoral Aid Society for a prayer from *Prayers for To-day's
Church* by Susan Williams.

SCM Press for prayers from *Contemporary Prayers for Public
Worship* ed. by Caryl Micklem and *The Primal Vision* by John V
Taylor.

SPCK for a prayer from *One Man's Prayers* by George Appleton.

Every effort has been made to trace the owners of copyright material,
and we hope that no copyright has been infringed. Pardon is sought
and apology made if the contrary be the case, and a correction will be
made in any reprint of this book.

Printed by Carlton Barclay Ltd.

Introduction

Jesus said: 'Ask, and it will be given to you; search, and you will find; knock, and the door will be opened to you. For the one who asks always receives; the one who searches always finds; the one who knocks will always have the door opened to him.' (Matt. 7:7-8)

How many times have you said yourself, or come across others who have said: 'But this is just not true: I've asked and asked and God never answers my prayer.'

As a result, some have given up believing in or trusting God. Others have found elaborate reasons for 'unanswered prayer'; yet others have said intercessory prayer is not valid and we should not ask God because he already knows our wants.

So what shall we say at the beginning of a book of intercessions? Surely, we must accept that throughout the history of the human race, men, women and children have asked things of each other, and of God. Surely, till the end of time, there is every probability that men, women and children will do the same. None of us need; many of us will.

What then do we ask for? If we are children, we ask almost without thinking; if we are friends, we open our need to our friend; if we really love each other, we expect and give more. Nothing need be barred from our asking

3

of God — except something wrong in itself. But God, who is far more loving than we are and far more wise, may see rightness and wrongness where we are blind.

Perhaps one of the deepest and most beautiful and difficult passages ever written about intercession is in relation to Jesus Christ's own prayer: 'During his life on earth, he offered up prayer and entreaty, aloud and in silent tears, to the one who had the power to save him out of death, and he submitted so humbly that his prayer was heard.' (Hebrews 5:7)

In using this little book, it would be good to
accept the loving fatherhood of God
open to him all our needs
allow him to love us.

Then we may indeed ask and receive, seek and find, knock and have the door opened because of our complete trust in God and Jesus Christ whom he has sent.

Our Intercessions

For all mankind
> O God, we pray
> > for bread for the hungry
> > homes for the homeless
> > peace for the fearful
> > healing for the sick
> > love for the hard of heart
> > life for the departed
> > > and Christ for all.

George Appleton
(One Man's Prayers, S.P.C.K.)

We pray for all mankind,
> Though divided into nations and races,
> Yet are all men thy children,
> Drawing from thee their life and being,
> Commanded by thee to obey thy laws,
> Each in accordance with the power to know and understand them.

Cause hatred and strife to vanish,
> That abiding peace may fill the earth,
> And humanity may everywhere be blessed with the fruit of peace.

So shall the spirit of brotherhood among men,
> Show forth their faith that
> Thou art the Father of all.

(Jewish prayer from the
Liberal Jewish Prayer Book)

For the Church

We pray for the Church throughout the world and particularly today for the Church in . . .

Unite all those who believe in your gospel and help them to understand each other better and teach them to respect the many ways there are of interpreting your message. In face of so much unbelief help us to stand together and co-operate with each other.

We are often confused because the ways of worshipping you as well as so much else is changing in your church; help us to hold firm to our faith in you who never change. And strengthen those who are persecuted for their faith so that they do not fall away at their time of testing.

We ask this in the name of your Son Jesus Christ who did not waver in time of trial.   Amen.

For our parish

Lord, give us grace to make this parish a place where everyone lives at peace with their neighbours and where all help each other without being organizing and domineering. Heal the sick if it be thy will, and strengthen the dying with the sense of your presence, and give us all joyful and thankful hearts. Amen.

God bless our church and parish,
and prosper all our attempts to be faithful
and to draw others to you,
for Jesus Christ's sake.   Amen.

For forgiveness of mankind

O Lord, forgive the cruelties of men of every age, their insensibility to other's pain, the deliberation that gives pain to satisfy and express the evil that rebels from love's surrender to other's needs to exalt itself.

O Lord, forgive the carelessness that passes by the blunted conscience that will not see or fear to see, the wrong men do to other men.

Most merciful, most loving Judge, Redeemer of mankind,
  Thou dost restore the fallen,
  Thou dost seek out the scattered sheep.

Gilbert Shaw

For our families

We pray for our families,
  with whom we live day by day.
May this most searching test of our character
  not find us broken and empty.
By all that we do and say
  help us to build up the faith and confidence
  of those we love.
When we quarrel help us to forgive quickly.
Help us to welcome new members into our families without reserve, and not to neglect whose who in our eyes have become less interesting and more demanding.

Contemporary Prayers for Public Worship

For those who hate

Lord, you prayed for those who were killing you. You had sympathy for them and you saw that they had no idea of the awfulness of the act they were committing.

So often we condemn and do not try to understand why people beat up, torture and kill others; we so often do not stop to pray for them; so now we beg you to open their eyes to the pain, bitterness and hate they cause. Heal them, and show them how inter-connected all people are.

Teach us to forgive those who injure us as you forgave those who were killing you, and prevent us from being self-righteous for our hardness of heart can cause others to become embittered.

Use us to bring love into the hearts of those who hate.

For those who neglect God

We pray for any who neglect you, Father;
    for any who have gone the wrong way,
    especially those who have brought trouble
    on themselves and others.

Take from them all blindness and stubborness.
Give them hope and strength to begin again.
And make other people loving and wise enough to help them.

Contemporary Prayers for Public Worship

For those with unpleasant work

Lord help those who have unpleasant and unrewarding work,
   those who are weighed down by great responsibilities,
   and those whose life is full of disappointment and who have little hope.
Lord, strengthen them so that they may bear their burdens bravely, and when possible give them companionship so that their loads may be lightened by being shared.
May our prayers and those of the saints be a help to them for we ask in the name of your Son, Jesus, who carries the burdens of the whole world.

For peace

Almighty God, from whom all thoughts of truth and peace do proceed: kindle, we pray you, in the hearts of all men the true love of peace, and guide with your pure and peaceable wisdom those who take council for the nations of the earth; that in tranquility your kingdom may go forward, till the earth is filled with the knowledge of your love, through Jesus Christ, our Lord.

Francis Paget, 1851-1911

A Disaster

Lord, help all those who have been hit by this disaster.

It seems inexplicable that so many are suffering loss, pain, and very great hardship. Today we are so very aware of being part of mankind and through radio and TV are conscious of the sufferings of those far from us; the knowing, seeing and hearing of their bewildered distress makes us feel so helpless.

All we can do just now is to ask you to comfort the orphans and widows, the bewildered, the hurt and the dying, and to give wisdom and strength to those near at hand so that they will give help wisely. Save the deprived from the temptation to loot, and preserve them from panic. Do not let the forces of evil take control.

We ask all this for the sake of your Son, Jesus Christ.

For the sick, the hungry, the lonely

Lord, comfort the sick, the hungry, the lonely and those who are hurt and shut in on themselves, by your presence in their hearts; use us to help them in a practical way.

Show us how to set about this and give us strength, tact and compassion.

Teach us how to be alongside them, and how to share in their distress in the depth of our being and in our prayer.

Make us open to them and give us courage to suffer with them, and that in so doing we share with you in the suffering of the world for we are your body on earth and you work through us.

For sailors

Protect, O Lord, your servants whose lives are spent on the oceans of the world. Guard them from all dangers, both of body and soul.

Strengthen them in their faith and give them courage never to deny it.

Grant them the grace to avoid all evil company, and never yield to bad example.

Lead them to repentance if they fall and, when called from this earth, may they enter the harbour of eternal life.

Help and inspire those who work for the good of seafarers to be united in their efforts for your greater glory, through Christ our Lord.

Denis McGuinness,
National Director of the Apostleship of the Sea.

For farmers

Let us pray for farmers; we depend on them for our daily food yet we forget the kind of work they do. It is often hard and messy. Your Son appreciated and understood the work of shepherds and farmers, but we so often take them for granted.

Help farmers in their work; encourage them to be concerned with the animals they look after; help them to take care of the land and not over-use it or damage it with dangerous chemicals which may destroy the birds, the insects and animals of the hedgerows. Give them strength, and the understanding of nature which we so often lack today.

For vandals

Lord we pray for the people we call vandals.
    They break windows,
    rip our telephones,
    slash railway carriage seats,
    for no reason we can understand.

Help us to see
    That we too commit
    acts of vandalism
    against your creation.

In the name of civilisation,
    we pollute rivers, the sea, the air,
    without thought or consideration
    of the damage we are doing.
    Help us and all vandals
    to learn to respect
    your creation and the good
    creations of mankind.
    Teach us to care for
    each other.
We ask this for the sake
of your Son. Amen.

For racial harmony

In a wonderful way you bring colours into the perfect
harmony of a rainbow.
    Help all the colours of the human rainbow to live in
peace and joy and harmony. Amen.

Wars

Lord, help those who are caught up in wars in this disturbed world, and especially just now we pray for . . . .

It is impossible for us to know the rights and wrongs of these wars, but we ask that you give the peoples involved the desire to reconsider their situations.

Give them more tolerance and understanding of each other; take the hatred and desire to dominate out of their hearts.

We ask this in the name of your Son who forgave and understood his enemies. Amen

Our multi-racial children

Children of all colours are happy together in their pre-school play-groups. Lord, may they never grow to a difference of feeling, let there be acceptance and love between black and white, white and brown and brown and black — for all are equal in your sight.

For unwanted children

O God, our Father, we remember before thee all orphaned, homeless and unwanted children, the children of loveless homes, and those who suffer from bodily defect and disease.

Make our hearts burn within us for the children of our dark places, and teach us how to turn to good account the laws that protect them and the efforts of those who strive to succour them;

through Jesus Christ our Lord.

Mothers' Union

For the hungry

O heavenly Father, who by thy blessed Son hast taught us to ask of thee our daily bread; have compassion on the millions of our fellow men who live in poverty and hunger; relieve their distress; make plain the way of help; and grant thy grace unto us all that we may bear each other's burden according to thy will; through Jesus Christ our Lord.

George Appleton

For the very old and tired

We pray for the old and tired who feel that they have lived too long and that no one wants them now.

Our own moments of loneliness teach us a little of their misery which must seem unending.

Help them to know that you love and care for them.

Teach them to rely more and more on you and fill their emptiness with your presence.

We ask this for the sake of your Son. Amen.

For those who are different

In your own life, Jesus, your gospel-writer tell us, you were very rude to a woman who was not a Jew and asked you to heal her daughter. You talked about giving the children's food to the dogs.

But her trust and faith won you over.

Can you teach us all to listen to the appeal of those who are different from us in race and faith — and be won over to welcome them to our table and our home.

To you, all people are equal in your love and care.
Teach us how to stop making some people more equal than others, because of their colour, creed or class.

God, why did you make us all so different?
Why do you allow us to hate and despise each other?
When will you answer Jesus' prayer
'that they all be one'?

Jesus — you died for everyone.
Help us to die to ourselves,
our prejudices, and our racialism. Amen.

Lord, make us colour blind.

For the unwanted

We pray for those who feel that they are unwanted and rejected by everyone, and for those who think their lives are pointless.

We are, in part, responsible for this slow kind of dying; help us to see each person we meet as worthwhile and as your son or daughter so that the unwanted may come to have a sense of belonging. It is terrifying to be friendless and forgotten.

Jesus, you were forsaken and rejected by men, but you cared for the outcasts of society; help us, your people, to show caring love to the neglected and unwanted.

Save our young people from feeling that their lives are useless and that all life is pointless. Teach us to love as you loved, we ask this in your name. Amen.

For our country

We beg you, Lord,
to improve the relationships
between young and old,
    whether they be black, white or brown.
Help those in the trouble spots of Britian
    to stop and think
    and not to resort to violence
    against those whom they see as enemies.

Give them understanding
    of other people's views,
    and take fear out of their hearts.

Prevent anarchy from breaking out in our land
    teach us all that violence breeds violence,
    and hatred leads to greater hate.
    Show us that in violent situations
    all lose their freedom to live as your creatures.

Let there be peace
so that we may live together
in the realisation that we are brothers and sisters,
and that you are our Father.

Race relations

Help us to appreciate the prejudices that people of
different colours and social backgrounds have for each
other. Here we rarely meet anyone of a different race and
when we do they seem pleasant and interesting.

Teach us how to pray for groups which fear and mis-
understand each other, and stop us from taking sides and
helping to increase the muddled kind of prejudice which
exists. Amen.

16

For the unemployed

Lord, how can we help the unemployed? It must be terrible to feel that no one wants your skills. It sounds lovely having nothing to do and it's OK for a little but it gets so boring. The feeling of being useless must be horrible. There must be ways of finding work for the unemployed for there seems to be so much that needs doing in the world.

Show us how to use ourselves and our resources; without your guidance we are lost.

The Divorced

O Lord, we pray for all those who, full of confidence and love, once chose a partner for life, and now are alone after final separation.

May they all receive the gift of time, so that hurt and bitterness may be redeemed by healing and love, personal weakness by your strength, inner despair by the joy of knowing you and serving others,

through Jesus Christ our Lord, Amen.

For suicides

Father of us all, have mercy on those who have taken their own lives. We do not know what tensions or what deprivations led them to this act. Help us to become more understanding and more loving to the lonely, the hurt, and unlovely of this world so that they will not take the same way out. And wrap those who have killed themselves in your love, so that they will live anew with you in your kingdom and come to glorify you, world without end. Amen.

17

Lord Christ, you accepted the gift of life in faith, and lived it out with courage; you can speak as no other in this anxious age, and teach us that courage comes in waiting patiently upon the Father.

Please give us that strong courage.

Please be with those who are lost, who simply do not know what they believe, and show them where they stand.

Please be with the anxious, who begin to despair even of life itself, and show them meaning.

Please be with those who are brought to the test, who feel tensions which rack the mind, and show them how to take one step in obedience and trust.

Please be with the sick who are held back from the life they would live, and give them hope and perfect healing.

Please be with those who do wrong, who steal and murder and destroy, and bring them through repentance to a new way of looking at things.

Please be with the bereaved, who are face to face with grim reality of death, and give them the generosity of spirit to entrust their lost ones into your living care.

Please be with all people who must live out their lives facing challenge as it comes, and speak strong words of courage to their troubled minds, that they may finish their course.

Through Jesus Christ, our Lord.

For those in distress

Lord Jesus, when you were on earth they brought the sick to you and you healed them all. Today we ask you to bless all those in sickness, in weakness and in pain;
> those who are blind and who cannot see the light of the sun, the beauty of the world, or the faces of their friends;
> those who are deaf and cannot hear the voices which speak to them;
> those who are helpless and who must lie in bed while others go out and in;
> Bless all such.
> those whose minds have lost their reason;
> those who are so nervous that they cannot cope with life;
> those who worry about everything:
> Bless all such.
> those who must face life under some handicap;
> those whose weakness means that they must always be careful;
> those who are lame and maimed and cannot enter into any of the strenuous activities or pleasures of life;
> those who have been crippled by accident, or by illness, or who were born with a weakness of body or mind:
> remember those who will never forget, because life for them can never again be the same.

This we ask for your love's sake.

William Barclay

May the souls of the faithful departed, through the mercy of God, rest in peace.

The dying

O Lord Jesus Christ, who in thy last agony didst commend thy spirit into the hands of thy heavenly Father: have mercy upon all sick and dying persons; may death be unto them the gate of everlasting life; and give them the assurance of thy presence even in the dark valley; for thy name's sake who art the resurrection and the life and to whom be glory for ever and ever.

Adapted from the
Sarum Primer

For the dead

Remember, O Lord, the souls of thy servants, who have gone before us with the sign of faith, and slumber and sleep in peace.

We beseech thee, O Lord, graciously to grant to them and all who rest in Christ a place of refreshment, light and peace; through the same Christ our Lord.

The Roman Canon

For those who mourn

We pray for those who mourn the loss of their dear ones. Comfort them and help them to know that we are all united with each other through your love.

We, too, remember those we love and those we have known who have left this earth and gone to your kingdom.

Help us and those recently bereaved to realise that our dead are in your keeping and that you love them and us with infinite love.

We ask this for the sake of your Son, Jesus Christ. Amen

My Intercessions

Surely the 'tender bridge' that joins the living and the dead in Christ is prayer? Mutual intercession is the life-blood of the fellowship, and what is there in a Christian's death that can possibly check its flow? To ask for the prayers of others in this life, and to know they rely on mine, does not show any lack of faith in the all sufficiency of God.

Then, in the same faith, let me ask for their prayers still, and offer mine for them, even when death has divided us. They pray for me, I believe, with clearer understanding, but I for them in ignorance, though still with love. And love, not knowledge, is substance of prayer.

J. Taylor,
'The Primal Vision'

Praying for others as they are in themselves

Lord, help me to pray for people not simply as they affect me, but for them as they are in themselves and in relationship to you.

It is so easy to ask you to make them love me, treat me with respect, and find me interesting.

Lord, help me to see them as people who also need love, respect, and interest, and forgive me my self-centredness.

Be in my relationship to them and bring us close to you.

For those I love

I bring before you those whom I love.
Watch over them, and keep them safe from all harm.
Amen

Help me to ask in faith

Lord, teach me to ask in faith.

I pray for wars to cease, but I am half-hearted because I don't believe man could stop being greedy so I think there will always be war.

I pray that people may become more loving and tolerant to each other, but I don't really think that they will change.

I pray for people to recover from their illnesses, or if they don't that they will grow more like you and will learn from their pain, but I ask half-heartedly, not believing.

Lord, increase my faith in you, your goodness and love, and help me really to believe in your power to work in others and in myself.

Save me from being cynical and give me faith as a grain of mustard seed which will grow and flourish.

Jesus, I ask this in your name.

For the world

Here I am on my own praying hiddenly for the world with all its problems which seem to take it by surprise. We misuse your gifts shockingly, so why should we be surprised when creation shocks us. We let evil, selfish desires take over us and our society and are amazed when terrible things happen.

I am praying that there may be more and more people who will let themselves be taken over by you and who will let your love flow through them to others, to the world, and so heal the tensions that surround us, and prevent the violence which spreads so quickly. Act through me and make me a channel for your love and peace. Amen.

Earthquake

Lord, help the people who are homeless now after the earthquake. Though I don't know them I can understand a little what it means to lose a house, furniture, pots and pans, and all the other things which belong to them and somehow give a sense of security. It must be a fearful thing to lose a home and loved ones in a few seconds.

Lord comfort them in their shattered world; stop them from panicking; and support them so that they don't feel completely hopeless. Give them strength to keep going, and show us how we can assist them and let them realise that others do care about their misery.

We ask this for the sake of Jesus Christ who gave himself for others.

For the distressed of the world

Lord, teach me to care for the suffering and distressed who are close to me in my street, in my village, in my work.

Show me how I can help them. Teach me through their misery to appreciate the sufferings of those in distant lands who seem so remote and difficult to pray for; help me to perceive the wonderful bond of love that links Christian people with all mankind and which aids us in bearing each other's burdens.

Make us more loving and considerate to each other, O Lord Jesus.

Make us brothers and sisters

I live in a city and we belong to every kind of colour and creed. The awful thing, Lord, is that we have deep prejudices against each other. We think badly and talk against each other. We do not really try to mix or come to know each other. Going along in our own groups, unconsciously we build barriers and foster deep dislikes and even hatred.

Send your unifying Spirit, Lord,
to melt and open our hearts;
to take away our selfish prejudices,
so that we rejoice in the varieties in your creation.
Make us brothers and sisters in the Lord.

An unhappy family

Lord, this family is divided and they are unhappy. I don't know what to do; I don't know the cause of the quarrel and perhaps even they have forgotten it themselves. There is a barrier of hate and fear between them. The children saw it as a game at first, but now it is making them miserable and they are becoming deceitful.

Stop this growing bitterness, and heal their wounds and put love in their hearts so that they may forgive and forget; show me how I can help for the sake of Jesus Christ, who forgave and healed so many people. Amen.

A bitter person

Lord, stop her from being bitter. She has been wronged certainly, but she is seeing more malice and heartlessness than there was in the situation.

Help her to forgive and to pray with understanding for the person who wronged her.

Give her that deep caring understanding which she did not receive herself; heal her wound with your love and put your love in her heart.

Make your love increase in all of us who are your followers so that we come to forgive each other as you forgive us.

For today's problems

I don't understand how people do the horrible things to each other which I read about in the newspapers. I find it hard to believe that they can torture each other the way they seem to because they have different political views or different religious beliefs. But eye-witnesses tell me it really happens.

Lord, I cry to you to help those who inflict such injuries.

Take hatred from their hearts; give them understanding of the evil they do.

Strengthen the persecuted; give them courage and a firm belief in you.

Give me and all who try to serve you the desire to serve the suffering and fill us with the love which will defeat the power of evil in the world. Amen.

I read the other day, Lord about some lion cubs. They were different from others because they were white.

I think their parents accepted them — did other tawny yellow lions look down on them or persecute them, Lord?

If so, then I hate this animal instinct, but if not why do we who are intelligent human animals – homosapiens – fear, hate, dislike and despise other humans who are coloured differently from us? Help us to be colour-blind, Lord.

You knew how to pray for your enemies; I don't know how to pray for football hooligans! They don't seem human to me! Give me understanding and show me how I should pray for them.

Lord, I know I should pray for our rulers, and statesmen and women, but they seem hopeless and beyond praying for. Yet I know quite well we have to pray for those who despitefully use us, and you never thought people were so bad as to be impossible to save. But didn't you have your doubts about the Pharisees? Probably you prayed about them a lot but the Bible doesn't tell us how.

Teach me how to pray for politicians and give me faith to keep on praying in the hopes that you will give them wisdom and eyes to see beyond their own party to the wider world and encourage them to work for the good of all mankind.

The lonely and those shut in on themselves

Lord, help the lonely especially those who find it difficult to communicate with others.

Teach me how to help them; how to approach those who are shut up in themselves, are afraid of other people, afraid of being laughed at, of being different.

Show me how to draw them out and make them talk and then to listen companionably.

Stop me from withdrawing into myself and giving up if I am snapped at when I try to break down barriers.

Those who care for the disabled

Lord I want to pray for those who spend their lives looking after the disabled. It is not easy for us to realise how much they have to give up to do this; ambition and high wages have to be put on one side so as to look after people whom many think are useless and shouldn't be kept alive.

Lord, help us to understand their devotion and their work. Give them your peace and strength so that they can keep on caring for the disabled lovingly and patiently, and also help them to accept that they will be despised as fools by the go-getters of the world. Teach them to learn from the courage of their patients when they are brave and cheerful, and in turn to be compassionate and understanding when their patients' limbs won't obey their minds even in very small things.

Open our eyes to the goodness in others.

For the busy

Lord, please bless and help people who are so busy working for you that they find little time to pray.

Give them strength to keep going and a sense that you are always with them and in their work.

Help them to realize that others, who have more time, pray for them and what they do, for in such ways we share with you in the bearing of each other's burdens.

My children

My children are far away from me and I think I have hurt them though I didn't mean to.

Wrap them in your love, the same love in which you hold me, and take away any bitterness from their hearts. They are in a strange place, without any roots, and insecure, so I beg you Lord to support and strengthen them and show them how much I love and care for them.

For a teenager in prison

He is in prison for life, Lord! In a way he has never had a chance — no parents, no home, no love, no God. Then he was in trouble, and on the run he killed a man . . . breaking in, Lord. He was hungry, you see. So what now? He knows the wrongness and regrets it deeply. He's been to the pit of despair, and now he's hunting for you, Lord. He wants you, and he wants to build anew, to know, to love, and to live.

Give him the courage and strength to live in that beastly place without further damage; give him light and hope and patience to go forward.

And Lord, give me the wisdom and warmth and patience and love to help him. Amen.

For a sick friend

He is ill and I don't know how ill, and he is a long way off.

Lord, strengthen him and give him courage and patience, and give me more faith so that I can trust whatever happens will be your will for him. Unite us, Lord, in our love for you and your love for us. I trust you but somehow let me know how he is.

I ask this for the sake of Jesus Christ who loved and cared for his earthly friends. Amen.

Lord, the one that I love is sick and in great pain; out of your compassion heal her and take away her pain.

It breaks my heart to see her suffer; may I not share her pain if it is not your will that she be healed? Lord, let her know that you are with her; support and help her that she may come to know you more deeply as a result of her suffering.

Lord be our strength and comfort in this time of darkness and give us that deep peace which comes from trusting you.

Help me believe you care

Lord, help me to believe that you really care for the people for whom I pray. I find it hard to trust you when so many unpleasant things seem to happen to them. It is not easy to understand how you can be watching over them in a caring way; increase my faith and show me how to pray. I ask this for the sake of your Son Jesus Christ.

For the deprived

Lord, I want to pray for the deprived who cannot pray themselves. It is hard for me who have the love and security of a family to understand how the deprived feel. I have creative work I enjoy, while they so often have dull mechanical jobs.

Help me to appreciate how being deprived can make people angry and violent. Stop me from hating those who are driven in desperation to violence for reasons I cannot understand. Use me to help those whose lives lack love and dignity. If I cannot do this at least give me the kind of love that is understanding and tolerant.

For a friend who is mentally distressed

Lord, how can I help my friend who is in such mental distress? I listen to him with as much sympathy as I seem to have.

Lord, without you I can do nothing. I have so little: like your apostles I present you my five loaves and two fishes but Lord, he needs so much more — there are five thousand of him. Help me, work through me with your spirit, make me understanding, sympathetic beyond my small capabilities and unendingly patient. Fill me with a love that is capable of this, and never let me count the cost beforehand.

Hear us, O Lord, thy sea is so large
and our boat is so small.

Welsh hymn.

Hurt in an accident

They have been in a motor accident, Lord. The hospital says they are all right though they ache all over. If they have any internal injuries, please heal them. It may have been his silly fault; he's a shocking driver and doesn't look after his car, but don't let him suffer any more, and don't let him drive again!

For the dead

I don't know how to pray for those whom I love and who are dead. If you are the God of love, you must love them too and cannot wish them to be hurt. Yet I know that they had many faults and did things which were wrong and you are just, as well as being merciful.

Lord, show me how to pray for them; I put them in your care and ask you for the sake of my love for them and for the sake of your Son, who loves mankind, to have mercy on them.

Ending Prayer.

I (God) am the ground of thy beseeching,
First, it is my will thou have it,
And then I make thee to will it,
And then I make thee to beseech it;
And if thou beseech it,
How should it then be that thou
    should not have thy beseeching?

Lady Julian of Norwich (b. 1342)